How to Prosper in Canada's Real Estate Crash

Kevin Bell

ARCHWAY
PUBLISHING

Archway Publishing books may be ordered through booksellers or by contacting:

Archway Publishing
1663 Liberty Drive
Bloomington, IN 47403
www.archwaypublishing.com
1 (888) 242-5904

ISBN: 978-1-4808-7544-9 (sc)
ISBN: 978-1-4808-7545-6 (e)

Library of Congress Control Number: 2019902993

Print information available on the last page.

Archway Publishing rev. date: 03/26/2019

Contents

Introduction

I wrote this book to help Canadians deal with the two biggest obstacles to their financial security - the tax man and financial advice that often stops and end with selling mutual funds.

I am not intending this to be a retirement book but a useful to reference guide when you are considering important financial decisions – from buying a house to investing, with a focus on reducing your taxes along the way.

By reducing investment management fees, avoiding a couple expensive financial mistakes, and using a simple strategy to reduce your taxes - it is very possible to achieve your financial goals.

Help is also available at www.kevinbell.ca

Chapter 1

Home Sweet Home

Although we could debate if housing qualifies as an investment, most people would agree that home ownership is a great way to build financial security, long term wealth, and secure a place to live. Many people consider their house their best investment.

After 25 years, you could own a house that is paid off and has increased in value significantly or you could have paid a lot of money in rent and have nothing to show for it.

For generations, homeownership has been a toehold on the ladder up for middle class Canadians, helping them build a nest egg and prepare for retirement. Young Canadians now find themselves priced out of high-priced cities, and often struggle to save for down payments or qualify for mortgages.

For first time home buyers, it is important to have a plan to guide you through the steps of buying a house. In Canada, there are three things you need to buy a house:

Credit

It is important to have an established credit history and understand your credit score. Lenders will need to see that you have established credit and a decent payment history before lending you money to buy a house. Some people mistakenly believe not using or having credit is a good thing but, it is not a good strategy if you need a mortgage to buy a house

Established credit means 2 credit lines (car payments, credit cards, lines of credit etc.) of at least $2,000 (for each credit line) reporting on your credit report for at least 2 years. For First Time Home Buyers there can be exceptions, for example for people who are new to Canada can be approved for mortgages with only 1 year of established credit.

The higher your credit score, the more financing options you have available. If your score is below 650 you can still get a good mortgage, but lending standards have tightened over the last couple years. Having a credit score above 700-720 will satisfy most mortgage lenders.

You can request your credit score and/or you can sign up for a credit monitoring program at Equifax.ca. Equifax is the standard used by all mortgage lenders in Canada.

It can be easy to improve your credit score, if you know what you are doing. I have an exclusive resource through The Mortgage Group who works with clients to quickly improve their credit score with a step by step plan. There are many unscrupulous providers of credit repair services, and if you need help in this area please save yourself some time and money by contacting Richard Moxley at eCredit Fix (richard@ecreditfix.ca).

Down Payment

In Canada, you are required to have a 5% down payment to purchase a house and this is the biggest obstacle for many

Canadians. The down payment is the portion of the purchase price that is paid by you and is due on your closing date.

There are programs available to help with down payments including RRSP loans and cash back mortgages. Not having a down payment does not need to be an obstacle to homeownership if you have good income and credit.

How much money do I need for a down payment?

- In Canada, your down payment can be as low as 5% of the purchase price of a home
- If your down payment is less than 20% of the purchase price, the mortgage is considered 'high ratio' and will need to be insured by CMHC, Genworth, or Canada Guarantee. Mortgage default insurance is an additional cost that is usually added to your mortgage balance. Mortgage default insurance is paid by the borrower and protects the lender in the event of default.

Where can I get the money for my down payment?

- A down payment can come from personal savings, RRSP's, TFSA's, a gift from family members or an inheritance, or some combination of these.
- The deposit you gave when you originally provided the offer on the property generally also becomes part of the down payment on closing.
- Lenders have a regulatory requirement (Anti-Money Laundering) which require them to verify that you have had the down payment in your possession for 90 days (unless it is a gift from a close relative). Often this can be one of the most administratively confusing documentation

requirements for completing a mortgage for first-time home buyers as large deposits during this 90-day period must be explained and documented for the lenders to satisfy these Anti-Money Laundering (AML) requirements.

What are the benefits of putting a 20% down payment?

- If you put a 20%+ down payment, your mortgage is considered "conventional" and you can avoid mortgage default insurance.
- Your mortgage balance and your mortgage payments will be lower
- You can use a 30-year amortization
- You can avoid the "stress test" by securing your mortgage with a provincially regulated credit union.
- Note - To purchase an investment property or property worth more than $1M, you are required to put down at least 20%.

Income

In Canada, the amount you can borrow for a mortgage is based on your income. Lenders and mortgage insurers each have very clear policies and definitions of how they calculate your income, depending if you are paid hourly or a salary, if you receive overtime and bonuses, child tax credit, have multiple employers, etc.

With the stress test, a reasonable rule of thumb is that you can get approved for a mortgage of approximately 5 times your gross annual income (s). You can be approved for more or less than this amount, depending on your existing debts, the property tax, and likely less if there are condo fees.

Again, the amount you can borrow is based on your income. Mortgage regulations allow 39% of your gross income to be allocated to house costs (mortgage payments, property taxes, heat, and condo fees, if any) and 44% of your income to all your debt payments (including all housing related costs mentioned and car payments, student loans, credit cards etc).

In the mortgage industry these 39% and 44% limits are known as a borrower's gross debt service (GDS) ratio and total debt service (TDS) ratio. While there may be small exceptions made on conventional mortgages, there are no exceptions made on these GDS/TDS ratios on insured mortgages.

Are there any benefits specifically for First Time Home Buyers?

As a first-time homebuyer, there are some programs that can save you some money along the way. The three big programs for first time homebuyers are land transfer tax rebates, home buyers tax credit, and Home Buyers Plan (HBP).

In some provinces and cities, there is a rebate available to help first-time homebuyers reduce the cost of the <u>land transfer tax</u>. If you qualify, land transfer tax rebates are available to first-time homebuyers in Ontario, British Columbia, and Prince Edward Island. There is also a land transfer tax rebate available for first-time homebuyers in the city of Toronto. For example, in Toronto, first time homebuyers are eligible for up to $3,725 in Toronto land transfer tax rebates in addition to up to $2,000 for first time homebuyers in Ontario ($5,725 Total).

The Home Buyers' Tax Credit works out to a rebate of $750 for all first-time buyers. After you buy your first home, the credit must be claimed within the year of purchase and it is non-refundable.

Kevin Bell

If you are purchasing a home with a spouse, partner or friend, the combined claim cannot exceed $750.

One great source of funding for your down payment is a Registered Retirement Savings Plan (RRSP). The Canadian government's Home Buyers' Plan (HBP) allows first time home buyers to borrow up to $25,000 from your RRSP for a down payment, tax-free. If you're purchasing with someone who is also a first time homebuyer, you can both access $25,000 from your RRSP for a combined total of $50,000.

One misconception is that you need to be a First Time Home Buyer to put down less than 20% to purchase a house. This is simply not true. Anyone can purchase a house as primary residence with less than 20% down, assuming the property is worth less than $1,000,000.

What is the Home Buyers' Plan?

The Home Buyers' Plan (HBP) is a program that allows you to withdraw up to $25,000 (per individual) from your registered retirement savings plans (RRSPs) to buy or build a <u>qualifying home</u> for yourself or for a related <u>person with a disability</u>.

Once the contribution have been in your RRSP for at least 90 days you can withdrawal the $25,000 under the Home Buyers Plan and use these towards your down payment.

Even if you or your spouse or common-law partner has previously owned a home, you may still be considered a first-time home buyer. It is also possible that only one of you is a first-time home buyer. You are considered a first-time home buyer if, in the <u>four year period</u>, you did not occupy a home that you or your current <u>spouse</u> or <u>common-law partner</u> owned.

Do you meet the RRSP withdrawal conditions?

- You have to be a <u>resident of Canada</u> at the time of the withdrawal.
- You have to receive or <u>be considered to have received</u>, all withdrawals in the same calendar year.
- You cannot withdraw more than $25,000.
- Only the person who is entitled to receive payments from the RRSP can withdraw funds from an RRSP. You can withdraw funds from more than one RRSP as long as you are the owner of each RRSP. Your RRSP issuer will not withhold tax on withdraw amounts of $25,000 or less.
- Normally, you will not be allowed to withdraw funds from a locked-in RRSP or a group RRSP.
- Your RRSP contributions must stay in the RRSP for at least 90 days before you can withdraw them under the HBP.
- Neither you nor your spouse or common-law partner can own the qualifying home more than 30 days before the withdrawal is made.
- You have to fill out <u>Form T1036, Home Buyers' Plan (HBP) Request to Withdraw Funds from an RRSP</u> for each eligible withdrawal.

Do you ever feel like you could spend your whole life saving money for a down payment?

When I first spoke with Tina and Jeremy early last year, they felt like they would never be able to save $25,000 for a 5% down payment on their $500,000 first home.

I explained that the federal government has a program for First Time Home Buyers, whereby they can each take $25,000 each out of their RRSP toward the purchase of home. In addition, I explained that banks are ready to lend them money to put into their RRSP and a $25,000 RRSP loan could be paid back over 10 years for about $275/month.

Since Tina and Jeremy were excited to get into their first house (things were getting stressful living with her parents) they completed the RRSP contribution before the March 1st RRSP deadline and also received almost $10,000 in tax refunds from Canada Revenue Agency that was used to cover closing costs (land transfer tax after rebates, lawyer fees, and movers) and also pay down some balances on Jeremy's credit cards.

As a mortgage broker, often clients and prospects reach out indicating that they don't have a down payment and won't be able to buy for years. Or more heartbreaking, is when clients run into real life situations where the down payment money they have been saving for years has been used for a family emergency.

With this strategy you (like Tina and Jeremy) will only need 90 days, which is how long the money needs to be in your RRSP prior to being withdrawn for the down payment towards the purchase of a house. The down payment money you already have saved can be used to reduce your other debts, reduce the amount you will need through an RRSP loan, or give you some financial flexibility in your first years of home ownership.

As an example, if you have $100,000 in combined family income (including child tax benefits) and a decent credit score, this strategy can have you moved into your own $500,000 home within 4 months.

Based on current interest rates for a $500,000 house, your monthly mortgage payment would be about $2,275/month and RRSP loan $275/month for a total monthly payment of $2,550.

But here's the bonus - since $1,150 of the mortgage payment is paying down principal, reducing the amount owing on your mortgage, and building equity in your home – <u>owning a $500,000</u>

home would be the equivalent of paying $1,400 ($2,550 - $1,150) in rent plus property taxes.

So, which way do you think is a better way to build long term wealth and secure a place to live – renting or owning?

Chapter 2

Home buying and mortgage details

If you are still reading, you likely agree that home ownership should be a top financial goal for most Canadians. There is help available to get young (and older) Canadians into the housing market and begin building wealth for the long term and securing a place to live at the same time.

There are a couple additional things to know if you are planning to buy a house and a couple ongoing questions (or debates) related to housing and personal finance including:

- Should I use a fixed or variable rate mortgage?
- Should I use a mortgage broker or a bank?
- Should I pay down my mortgage or invest in an RRSP (or TFSA etc.)

There have been many changes related to mortgages over recent years from the "stress test" to interest rates gradually increasing. For homebuyers and homeowner, the first challenge is to understand are the types of mortgages available in Canada.

Getting the best mortgage rate in Canada now depends on your type of mortgage. With the recent regulatory changes in the

Canadian mortgage market, there are now 3 types of mortgages. These are insured mortgages, insurable mortgages, and uninsurable mortgages.

The **<u>absolute</u> best rates are for mortgages that are insured** by one of the 3 Canadian mortgage default insurance companies: CMHC, Genworth or Canada Guarantee. The borrower pays for mortgage default insurance, which is usually added to the mortgage balance. The lender benefits since they have little or no risk for their money, since the mortgage is insured against default. In addition, the lender is also now able to securitize and sell these mortgages to investors.

Insured – lowest interest rates

- All home purchases with less than 20% down payment
- Property value must be below $1 Million dollars
- Maximum 25-year amortization
- Cannot be a rental property
- Must qualify with Stress Test (Bank of Canada rate, or 2% higher than the mortgage contract rate)

Insurable - often higher rates than insured rates

- Same Insured Criteria as above but -
- Home purchases with more than 20% down payment

Uninsurable – often higher rates than insurable rates

- Rental properties
- Refinances or equity-take-outs
- Properties valued over $1 Million dollars
- Amortizations greater than 25 years

Insured mortgages can be securitized and sold, which reduces the lenders capital requirements. In addition, lenders are protected from a potential default of the borrower.

Insurable mortgages can be insured by the lender, then securitized and sold to reduce capital requirements. Lenders generally charge a higher rate than for insurable mortgages since they will either be paying for the default insurance or accepting the risk of borrower default.

For uninsurable mortgages, the lenders need to be compensated for the added risk of holding a mortgage without default insurance and the additional capital requirements for the lender. With uninsurable mortgages, the borrower pays for the higher risk and capital requirements in the form of higher interest rates.

Borrowers who have diligently saved 20% or more for a down-payment in some ways feel penalized in the form of a higher interest rate as the borrowers putting less than 20% down gets rewarded with the best rates available (but remember they have the added expense of the default insurance).

Here is how it plays out in real life. Assume three neighbors in Toronto live in a neighborhood where housing prices are very close to $1,000,000.

John and Andrea find a house and purchase it from $990,000, they put down the minimum down payment, which in this case is $74,0000. The minimum down payment is 5% on the first $500,000 ($25,000) purchase price and 10% on the remaining $490,000 ($49,000).

The total mortgage loan amount will be $952,640 which is calculated at $990,000 purchase price minus the $74,000 down payment plus the $36,640 cost of the mortgage default insurance.

Note the mortgage default insurance is calculated as 4% of the mortgage for buyers putting down less than 10% (like John and Andrea), 3.1% of the mortgage amount for buyers putting down up to 15%, and 2.8% of the mortgage amount for buyers putting down less than 20%.

John and Andrea, with the help of a mortgage broker secure a 5-year fixed rate "insured" mortgage through an insurance company, with a great rate of 3.29% (ensuring a low Interest rate differential calculation if they sell before the end of their 5-year term). The monthly payments work out to be $4,651.27.

Our second couple Steve and Ali purchase the neighboring house for the same price ($990,000) but decide to put down 20%. Since the house will be their primary residence, is worth less than $1M, and Steve and Ali decide to use a 25-year amortization the mortgage is "insurable".

Through a monoline mortgage lender, with the help of a mortgage broker Steve and Ali are offered 5-year fixed rate of 3.49%. The total mortgage amount is $792,000 (80% of the purchase price since no default insurance premium is added) and the monthly payment is $3,950.04.

Our third couple, Kris and Melissa, have been living in the house next door for 5 year already and at the end of the original mortgage term decided to refinance taking equity from their property to consolidate debt, top up investment accounts and help a family member in need. A refinance is uninsurable

Kris and Melissa secured a 5-year fixed rate mortgage with their bank, since they were very confident, they wouldn't break the mortgage before the end of the term and be required to pay the banks IRD calculation, they secured their mortgage through their local bank.

Through a bank, with the help of a mortgage broker that explained how the potential breakage penalty was calculated Kris and Melissa are offered 5-year fixed rate of 3.79%. The total mortgage amount is $792,000 (80% of the purchase price since no default insurance premium is added) which is the same as Steve and Ali, but the monthly payment is $4,076.41.

The monthly payment was $126.37 higher than Steve and Ali.

John and Andrea's mortgage was "insured" and the rate was 3.29%, Steve and Ali's mortgage was "insurable" and the rate was 3.49%, Kris and Melissa's mortgage was "uninsurable" and the rate was 3.79%. This is how the mortgage market in Canada works in 2019.

As a mortgage broker, clients will often want to know what the rate is for a mortgage and it is not a simple question to answer anymore. The days of having a single rate for all mortgage types are gone, and often the best rates can be quite different depending if the mortgage is insured, insurable, or uninsurable.

Fixed or variable?

In addition to insured, insurable, and uninsurable mortgages, there are many products in the mortgage market from lines of credit, interest only mortgages, and different terms (1, 2, 3, 4, 5, 10 years etc.), but for most borrowers the question with respect to interest rates is – fixed or variable?

My experience is that in very few cases does it make sense to explore anything other than using a 5-year fixed or 5-year variable rate mortgage for your primary residence. Many lenders will allow the mortgage to be split into segments with half fixed rate and half variable rate components for those who can't decide.

With a 5-year fixed rate mortgage, your (monthly, weekly, or biweekly) payment is known with certainty for the next 60 months based on the interest rate and amortization you agree to with your lender. With a 5-year variable rate mortgage your monthly payment is variable, it could increase or decrease, depending on changes to your lenders prime rate.

Generally, variable rates mortgages offer (initially at least) lower rates and payments than for fixed rate mortgages.

For variable rate mortgages, the interest rate changes each time lenders change their Prime rate. Lenders change their Prime rate when the Bank of Canada changes the Overnight Rate by increasing or decreasing interest rates.

For example, in November 2018 the Bank of Canada raised their Overnight Rate by 0.25% to 1.75% from 1.50% and mortgage lenders in Canada raised their Prime Rates from 3.70% to 3.95%

Borrowers typically are offered a discount to prime, so for a borrower that had agreed to pay the bank Prime minus 1% for a 5-year term, the interest rate on his mortgage would increase from 2.70% to 2.95%, and generally the remaining mortgage payments would also increase as a result.

Note – TD Bank has a special Mortgage Prime interest rate that is 0.15% higher than all other lenders (currently 4.10%). One other difference with TD Bank is that the payments on variable rate mortgages do not change with changes to interest rates. The higher rates instead increase the amortization (time it will take to pay back) the mortgage, and lower rates decrease the amortization of the mortgage.

Now, you might think, that having a payment that changes vs. one that doesn't is the key difference between fixed and variable rate mortgages. It is not.

The biggest difference between fixed and variable rate mortgages is how the penalties are calculated if the mortgage is paid out early. The majority of mortgages in Canada are renegotiated before the end of the term and there can be a variety of good reasons for this – from pursuing better employment opportunities elsewhere, to upsizing/downsizing, death, divorce, refinancing to access equity to invest, renovate, or consolidate debt.

With a variable rate mortgage, the penalty to payout the mortgage in full is typically calculated as 3 months interest. With fixed rate mortgages the penalty can be much more severe.

Have you ever wondered why banks have such ridiculous mortgage rates?

The Interest Rate Differential (IRD), is a prepayment penalty, levied by lenders if you pay off your fixed rate mortgage before it matures or if you pay off principal, beyond the amount allowed by your prepayment privilege.

On variable-rate mortgages the prepayment penalty is usually three months interest, with the exception of lenders that offer "no frills" mortgages often to unsuspecting client that only care about the rate. However, with a fixed-rate mortgages, the penalty is usually the greater of three months interest or the Interest Rate Differential (IRD).

The IRD is based on: The amount you are pre-paying; and, an interest rate difference between your original mortgage interest rate and the interest rate that the lender can charge today when lending the funds for the remaining term of the mortgage.

For example, with a 5-year 3.5% fixed rate mortgage, you promised the lender to pay 3.5% for five years. If you decide to break that arrangement after three years the lender gets the remaining money back to re-lend. To match the original term, the lender wants to get the same interest rate on the remaining two years.

Lender will calculate how much less interest they will receive over the remaining term at the lower reinvestment rate compared to your promise of 3.5%. Assuming the reinvestment rate is close to 3.5%, you would pay three months interest penalty.

The big difference between big banks and non-bank lenders (monoline mortgage lenders, credit unions, insurance companies) is that the non-bank lenders calculate the difference between your original interest rate and the current interest rate for the remaining term, generally resulting in a penalty of 3 months interest.

The banks calculate IRD differently. If the original "posted" rate was 5.5% but your friendly banker got you a discount and only charged you 3.5%, the IRD would be calculated between 5.5% and the reinvestment rate, which increases the penalty massively. In this example, (5.5%-3.5%) 2% per year for the remaining term of the mortgage.

In my practice as mortgage broker, I could tell you heartbreaking stories about families being severely impacted by a banks IRD calculation. One client paid over $40,000 to discharge a $1M mortgage when the house was sold after the sudden and unexpected death of her husband (primary bread winner). Death, divorce, and other family emergencies happen in real life and my best advice is that if you are certain you want a fixed rate mortgage, you want to avoid Canadian banks and call a qualified mortgage broker.

Bank or Broker - What's best for consumers?

I can't overstate the impact of someone's personal finances of paying tens of thousands of dollars in a confusing and poorly disclosed penalty to a bank that generates billions of dollars in profit each year, but I can tell you this is the kind of financial mistake that people only make once in a lifetime.

The fact is that over 60% of mortgages in Canada are

renegotiated before the end the term. Do yourself a huge favour and call a broker if you are ever considering a fixed rate mortgage.

The basic difference between a bank mortgage specialist and an independent mortgage broker comes down to providing choice for consumers. If you walk into a Toyota dealership, don't be surprised if the car that the specialist recommends for you is a Toyota.

In addition to having access (directly or indirectly) to the major Tier 1 banks in Canada, mortgage brokers also have access to many other provincially-regulated and private mortgage lenders. Those lenders include credit unions (Meridian, Duca, etc.), insurance companies (Desjardins, Manulife, etc), monoline mortgage lenders who have funded hundreds of billions of dollars in aggregate (including First National, MCAP, Merix, Street Capital, etc.) alternative lenders (Equitable, Home Trust, etc.) and private lenders.

Choice allows brokers to ensure that the features of the mortgage are aligned to the client's needs. Brokers will look at pre-payment options, how penalties are calculated, how the mortgage is registered and how the client credit fits against the available products in the market. The broker shops the market to secure the lowest overall cost of borrowing for the unique needs of each consumer. Competition maximizes the opportunity for a consumer to get the best overall deal through a mortgage broker.

Brokers deal with large banks and sometimes banks provide the best option for a client. Other times specialty lenders, mono-line lenders, insurance companies and credit unions will provide the best options for a client. Broker market share has increased steadily since the Global Financial Crisis and with each additional mortgage rule and regulation changes brokers are best suited to independently assess a mortgage client's needs and then access all available market options to fit those needs.

A recent Bank of Canada survey found that -

"The results indicate that borrowers who use a mortgage broker pay less, on average, than borrowers who negotiate with lenders directly. This average discount is about an additional 19 basis points."

Most mortgage brokers offer ongoing advice and information to their clients. Because they deal with a wide variety of lenders for unique circumstances they are often very well versed in issues affecting mortgage borrowers.

For example, a bank mortgage specialist may tell you all un-insured mortgages have to be qualified at the benchmark rate or 200 basis points (whichever is higher). What they mean to say is all their bank mortgages are qualified in that manner. Other lenders, credit unions for example, can still qualify the borrower at the contract rate. Brokers take the time to first understand a client's needs, both short term and long term, then recommend the right mortgage and present options.

By working with a licensed mortgage professional, you have a trusted advisor and problem solver, who is best positioned to present all your options. As the lending environment changes, brokers keep up-to-date with all these changes and have access to a variety of lenders including banks, credit unions, trust companies, monoline lenders and private lenders.

Another key differentiator is the service level you can expect from a great mortgage broker. Throughout the life of a 5-year mortgage, there may be opportunities to switch your mortgage to another lender and save money.

Last summer a couple of lenders began offering discounts on variable rate mortgages of Prime minus 1% and lower in some cases. Many clients that were only a couple years into a 5-year fixed rate mortgage at prime minus 0.3%, as discounts to Prime were much small in previous years.

These clients would save 0.7% on each remaining year by refinancing, which in some cases was up to 3.5% or 4% of the remaining mortgage balance. This refinancing strategy generally required paying a 3-month interest penalty (these were usually about 0.7% to 0.8% of the mortgage balance) and doing about an hour of paperwork.

If you get a mortgage with a bank, don't expect them to call you when you can save tens of thousands of dollars by refinancing, either with them or another lender. With the help of a great mortgage broker, market changes will create opportunities to save money on your mortgage.

Other Potential Pitfalls

Since it is worth repeating, easily the most avoidable and common mistake Canadians make is getting a fixed rate mortgage with a Canadian Bank.

The second things Canadians do instinctively is focus exclusively on rates believing that terms between lenders are the same. The result is that many lenders now offer what are referred to as "no frills" mortgages, generally these come with restrictive terms and much bigger penalties. Believe me when I tell you the lenders have done the math on the products and borrowers don't win by agreeing to a mortgage with a big penalty (especially when most mortgages are refinanced).

If you are shopping for a mortgage on the internet and your only criteria is getting the lowest rate, be careful because you might get what you are asking for.

In a disturbing development some lenders (including Bank of Montreal and Meridian Credit Union) include a Bona-fide Sales Clause with some discounted mortgages. A bona-fide sales clause means you can't payoff your mortgage during the term unless you sell the property. You want to run from any lender that includes this clause in a mortgage commitment.

Paying down mortgage or contribute to an RRSP?

Like many great debates there may not be a single right answer, but ultimately whether you should pay down your mortgage or contribute to your RRSP depends on your risk tolerance.

The primary advantages of using an RRSP are (1) the immediate tax deduction for the contribution and (2) the ability to compound investment growth tax free.

The immediate tax deduction often provides an immediate tax refund. Whether the tax refund is a net financial benefit over your lifetime depends on two factors. First, your marginal tax rate at the time you are contributing to your RRSP compared to your marginal tax rate at the time of withdrawal. Second, since you get use of the tax refund for the entire period until you withdraw the funds from your RRSP, the time value of the tax savings also plays a role.

There is a great deal of uncertainty around estimating what your marginal tax rate will be in retirement. Tax rates are always changing and estimating your income at some distant date in the future is impossible, but conventional thinking on RRSP's is that people generally face lower marginal tax rates in retirement.

Since both growth within RRSP's and gains on principal residence are tax free. The question is really "can you generate returns inside your RRSP greater than the interest rate you pay on your mortgage?".

Paying down your mortgage offers an immediate, guaranteed, after tax return equal to the interest rate on your mortgage. With current mortgages rates the bar isn't too high to finding diversified investments offering much greater expected returns.

As long as your RRSP investments have an expected return above your existing mortgage rate, it makes sense to contribute to your RRSP. Generally, you should not be investing in assets with a lower expected return than your current mortgage interest rate inside your RRSP.

If you have other debt, you should compare the highest interest rate you pay with how much you expect to earn on your investments, to see if investing in your RRSP makes sense. Paying down_debt provides an immediate after-tax return equal to the interest rate on the debt.

Mortgage Life Insurance

Life insurance is a separate and important discussion and beyond the scope of this book.

Life insurance is one of the first financial discussion to have and should involve a qualified life insurance agent, who can take you through a need analysis and determine what coverage is best. Life insurance should be considered for your loans, replace your income (if you have dependents), cover your final expense.

Banks will often try to sell life insurance with mortgages. You should always say NO to mortgage insurance and look for a term policy instead, and here's why ...

- Mortgage insurance is creditor insurance (it is not life insurance), which means that the proceeds go to pay off your mortgage. Paying off your mortgage may not be the only way your beneficiaries would like to use the life insurance proceeds.

- With term insurance, your overall health is taken into account and non-smokers receive better rates vs. with mortgage insurance which depends only on your age. Term insurance is generally much less costly than mortgage insurance.

- With term insurance, you choose how much coverage you need and your coverage remains level throughout the term of your policy vs. with mortgage insurance where coverage reduces as your mortgage is paid down.

- A term insurance policy belongs to you and is fully portable. If you change mortgage provider, or your health changes, your coverage travels with you.

- With term insurance the policy is underwritten when you apply and you have full knowledge that your policy will protect your loved ones vs. with mortgage insurance, which determines if you have coverage after a claim has been made. If the lender finds any discrepancies on your initial application or investigating your medical history, your claim could be denied.

Chapter 3

Canada housing bubble

In recent years, there have been many market commentators and analyst asked whether Canada is in a housing bubble. Since that is a question that I often get from many home buyers, real estate investors, and real estate agents. Here is my view -

Impact of regulatory changes

A December 2018 report from the Bank of Canada reviewed the impact of the government's policy changes on the mortgage market. The Bank of Canada found that overall market activity had slowed - something most everyone expected would happen eventually since that was the goal of the policy changes.

Put differently, if the housing market and debt levels did not slow, additional policies would have likely been introduced to slow the market since that is what the policy makers were trying to achieve in the first place.

The Bank of Canada's data shows a slowdown in "riskier" mortgages which they defined as having more than have a high (above 4.5 times) mortgage to income ratio as a result of these changes.

The Bank of Canada patted itself on the back for the good work they had done to protect the financial system.

The reality is that many of these borrowers have turned to the unregulated mortgage market as these (high debt to income) mortgages are no longer allowed within the regulated banking world.

History of Mortgage Lending Changes

In 2016, the Office of the Superintendent of Financial Institutions (OSFI) announced a stress test for insured mortgages (mortgages with less than 20% down and requiring mortgage default insurance), stipulating that those buyers must qualify at the Benchmark rate (currently 5.34%) using the same 39/44 Gross Debt Service/Total Debt Service ratios described previously.

In October 2017, a similar rule was unveiled for uninsured mortgages (mortgages with more than 20% down payment) stipulating that those buyers must qualify at either 2% more than the contracted mortgage rate or the Benchmark rate, whichever is higher.

These two rule changes known as the "stress test", along with several others, including increasing minimum down payments, mortgage default insurance premium hikes, and decreasing amortization limits, have made it harder for Canadians to qualify for mortgages.

The rationale for these policy changes was to encourage people to take on less overall debt, including less mortgage debt, which would (in theory at least) keep the housing markets safe by protecting borrowers in the event interest rates increased and by protecting lenders from borrowers being unable to service debts and from falling house prices.

The Fallout

Clients who qualified for an "A" mortgage immediately qualified for only about 80% of what would have previously been approved as a result of the "stress test". By October 2017, this impacted all regulated mortgages in Canada.

It is important to understand that with very few exceptions in Canada's regulated mortgage market, the size of the mortgage that can be approved is determined by the applicant's income (not the value of the property). In Canada, a mortgage is a loan against your income, not a loan against the value of your house.

Many high-quality borrowers shifted down the ladder to lenders with a higher risk tolerance and more flexible lending policies. These mortgages of course come with higher interest rates. Borrowers who don't fit into the mainstream box are not limited to those with past credit issues, and may include self-employed, those who are new to Canada, and previously "A" clients with excellent credit but lower incomes.

Alternative mortgage lenders also known as "B" lenders, are more willing to look at each situation on a case-by-case basis and consider a borrower's "story". For example, if a borrower had a bankruptcy or previous credit issues, they want to know the story behind it in order to assess whether it is likely to occur again.

In addition, B lenders typically have more flexible income definitions than A lenders. For example, with self-employed borrowers or borrowers that rely on tips, B lenders will consider bank statements to demonstrate income rather than exclusively focus on tax returns as is typically the case in the "A" space.

The Unregulated Market

The unregulated market is primarily comprised of private mortgage lenders – companies, individuals, and mortgage investment corporations (MICs) -- who fall outside the purview of Canada's banking regulators. Private lenders offer mortgage rates much higher than traditional mortgage lenders and for shorter terms.

Borrowers who could not qualify for traditional lending turned to these alternative and private lenders. Private lenders are less concerned with an applicant's credit or income and much more focussed on the value of the property. The lender wants a cushion between what they are owed and what the property can be sold for, in the event the borrower stops paying the mortgage.

As a result of the rule changes, alternative lenders saw an uptick in business as credit worthy mortgages clients are now often required to explore borrowing options in the unregulated space.

The Bank of Canada acknowledges that this segment of mortgage lending is growing. The bank indicated that the market share for private lenders in the GTA has grown by 50% from 2017 to 2018, and now makes up nearly one out of every 10 borrowers.

There are now questions about risk in the unregulated market.

Is there cause for concern?

There can be many reasons to access short term funding in the private lending space. But let's be clear, in the world of private lending a first mortgage would approach 10% when interest rates and fees are included, and second mortgages generally start at 12%.

Sometimes clients will need to consolidate debts in order to lower monthly payments or improve their credit score in order to qualify for a better mortgage in the future. Sometimes borrowers will face a huge IRD penalty and higher interest rates to refinance a bank mortgage and will borrow privately until the existing mortgage is due.

Whatever the reason for accessing an alternative lender, private lending is not a long-term solution. With private lending t is critical to have an "exit strategy". If you have a private mortgage, and you don't know exactly when and how you are moving back into a better mortgage than you need a much better mortgage broker.

If 10% of borrowers are using private lending, alarm bells should be ringing at the Bank of Canada and financial regulators in Canada. As borrowers rely on the private funds for longer periods, this will have a destructive impact on the borrower's financial health.

In real life

Simone had contacted me last year to enlist my help to reduce the interest she is paying on her private mortgage and her story is representative of the pitfalls of accessing private lending and why I believe it is a certainty that many of the overheated markets in Canada are headed for a meaningful correction.

In 2018, Simone had a good job, making in excess of $100,000 annually, was single and had a habit of spending more than she made (not a recipe for long term financial success). There were unexpected expenses along the way that compounded some of her financial issues.

Simone had purchased a condo for $390,000 in 2014 that had risen in value substantially since she purchased it. In 2016 she had refinanced successfully with an A lender to consolidate some debt she had on credit cards. In 2017, she had taken out a $50,000 private mortgage behind her bank mortgage based on a $600,000 appraisal of her condo. She had borrowed $480,000 on a condo that she purchased for $390,000 only 4 year earlier.

Simone had just leased a BMW and had another $20,000 that she would like to consolidate into her mortgages.

The first problem was that with car payments, condo fees, and mortgage, even with her income the TDS ratio was tight. In addition, with the $20,000 which was close to the maximum of her 4 credit cards her credit score had taken a beating.

The second problem was that there was now little to no equity in her condo, since values in her area had started to fall. Her appraisal came in at $550,000 and there are no worthwhile mortgage lending options to go above 80% of the value of her property, which meant that she couldn't even payout her mortgages, never mind the consumer debt.

Short of winning the lottery, Simone's best financial option is to sell her property. It is also her only realistic option. But Simone like thousands of homeowners in the GTA/GVA is planning to wait out the market. Simone and many others currently believe that if they hold on long enough, the market will resume it's inevitable upward trajectory and she will be able to refinance and payout all her debts at a lower rate.

There is a private lender that has been charging 15% for her $50,000 second mortgage and collecting $625/month in interest every month, meanwhile the principal on her loan has not been reduced by a penny. When the mortgage comes due in the summer, renewing the private mortgage will be an issue.

The lender is no doubt aware of a lengthy, expensive, and complicated legal process to force a sale of the property, and during that time values could continue to fall. In addition to falling market values, I wouldn't expect the property to be ready for showings by the time the proud current owner vacates. There will also be commission paid to a real estate agent to facilitate the sale.

There are many people who have paid living expenses through the 25-year bull market in real estate by accessing the equity in their homes. This is only possible when property values increase, when values decrease the system starts to fall apart quickly.

Regulatory Capture

Regulatory capture is a form of policy failure which occurs when a regulatory body, created to act in the public interest, advances the commercial interests of the industry it is charged with regulating.

In Canada, regulators have repeatedly prevented meaningful competition, from foreign companies to technology start ups, from entering the financial service space in Canada. It is also my view that regulators have taken steps to advance Canada's big bank interests ahead of the public interest in financial service regulation. Look no further than the mortgage rules that have been introduced recently.

First, when regulators determined that mortgage refinances (meaning increasing mortgage balance or extending the amortization), rental properties, 30-year amortization, and properties over $1M could not be insured they eliminated an important source of capital and competition for these types of mortgages.

Monoline mortgage lenders had relied on the mortgage default insurance, and subsequent securitization and sale of the insured mortgage pools, to compete effectively with banks for these types of mortgages. Banks have much larger balance sheets and typically lend from their own capital and can now do so with reduced competition as monolines mortgage lenders can no longer compete.

Instead, today all monoline mortgage lenders are aggressively focussed on growing their alternative lending businesses.

Second, the introduction of the "stress test" immediately reduced each borrowers capacity to borrow by ~20%, while interest rate increases have reduced each borrower's capacity by an additional ~10%. The result is that many borrowers do not have enough income to qualify for the mortgage that they already have.

On renewal, these borrowers have limited options and are usually required to accept whatever rate is on the renewal offer is from there existing lender. Since banks have steadily seen falling market share in mortgage origination as borrowers increasingly enlist the service of mortgage brokers, the bank regulators have implemented the stress test in a way to allow the banks access to maintain exclusive high margin business.

Effectively, your bank can charge you whatever they want on your mortgage renewal when they know you can't leave.

Credit and Debt

Credit is buying power, which is generally good in that it facilitates economic transactions. The buying power is given in exchange for a promise to pay it back which is called debt. Most of what Canadians consider money is really credit.

When a bank advances a mortgage (or any loan) money is created. With a mortgage, the house seller receives the money and the buyer has a debt to repay.

The question on whether credit and debt growth is good or bad depends on what the credit produces and how the debt is repaid. Generally, because credit creates both spending power and debt, whether more credit is good depends on whether the borrowed money is used productively enough to generate enough income to service the debt.

Canada's Housing Bubble

Bubbles generally start with fundamentally driven bull markets. In Canada, housing market fundamentals including low and stable interest rates and ongoing immigration. Strong and stable economic conditions have supported increasing home prices for close to 25 years.

As home prices increased net worth and income levels increased, and confidence supported additional borrowing and spending. The housing boom encouraged new buyers into the market who didn't want to miss out on the action (FOMO), often pulling purchase decisions forward.

As new speculators and additional lenders entered the market, confidence increases and credit standards fall, allowing for more market participants, more people to enter the market further supporting demand and confirming the boom.

Rising house prices lead to more spending and more buying, which raises house prices further. Everyone wants to own a house and eventually everyone who wants to own a house already owns a house, and many have borrowed as much as they can to buy a house, often to buy as many houses as they can.

The following is something I posted on LinkedIn the day the first stress test was introduced for insured mortgages.

Effective today (October 17ᵗʰ, 2016) all insured mortgages with a down payment of less than 20% will need to qualify at the greater of either the Bank of Canada benchmark rate (4.64%) or the contract rate offered on their mortgage commitment. For reference, a five year fixed rate mortgages are currently available at 2.19% (less than half the "stress test" benchmark rate).

What this does policy means to the average Canadian family and the average Canadian house price? In short, it means that unless an average family has $100,000 for a down payment (and closing costs) they can no longer afford an 'average' house.

The average Canadian family earns $82,056/year and the average price of a house in Canada is $474,590.

If we assumed the average family had a great credit history, no car payments, no credit card debt, or no other borrowing (and assuming property taxes of 1% of the purchase price of the house) that family could have qualified to purchase a property for $570,000, until October 17ᵗʰ.

After October 17ᵗʰ, by requiring this family to qualify at the benchmark rate of 4.64% they can now afford to purchase a property only worth $457,500.

What happens when an 'average' Canadian family can no longer afford an 'average' house?

Availability of credit certainly plays a role in residential real estate prices and it is likely we are entering a period in Canada (with this policy and more to come) where credit growth will be lower than income growth. The value of residential real estate plays an important role in how households perceive their wealth, and that perception impacts decisions regarding household consumptions, savings and investments.

We are starting to see some issues with the market including asset-liability mismatches (private lending), as people like Simone take short term loans to buy long term and often illiquid real estate and others invest in riskier debt (private lending) and assets (including MIC's) with borrowed money.

Debt to income ratios have increased rapidly in Canada.

As debts have risen, the cost to service those debts has risen even faster. In Canada that is the double whammy of higher interest rates and tighter mortgage regulations.

Now we are starting to see tighter lending policies from all mortgage lenders who are increasingly concerned with credit scores, a borrower's other assets, and additional limitations on the types of properties they will consider reducing lending further.

Monetary policy helped inflate the bubble by keeping interest rates at record low levels. It is important to recognize that the Bank of Canada has a single mandate in Canada which is to keep inflation within a 1 to 3% target band. The Bank of Canada does not target debt levels or house prices.

Canada's housing bubble has popped despite what your real estate board may indicate. Now falling asset prices decrease the owner's equity and collateral values and which cause lenders to pull back further. This forces speculators to sell, driving down prices even more.

Ray Dalio from Bridgewater Associates has developed a list of defining characteristics of bubbles from prices being high relative to traditional measures, prices are expecting further appreciation from these levels, bullish sentiment, purchases being financed by high leverage, buyers who have made forward purchase, new buyers entering the market, and stimilative monetary policy.

It would be easy to make a case that all of these elements were present in Canada as real estate prices peaked in early 2017 with house prices high relative to historic rents and income measures, borrowers purchasing negative cash flow investments and banking on further appreciation, housing becoming a regular topic of water cooler conversation, the sharp increase in use of private mortgages, buyers purchasing preconstruction investment properties, people entering the market who have seen friends and family's houses increase in value (FOMO), and stimilative monetary policy from record low interest rates.

From data since the introduction of the foreign buyers, tax we can see that foreign buyers were also very active in many urban markets, Toronto and Vancouver specifically.

Mortgage fraud has also been a driver of additional borrowing. In my daily business, I have had many mortgage prospects indicate that banks fabricated income documentation in order to get mortgages and these clients would not qualify for the mortgages otherwise. The fee to arrange one of the mortgages was 1 or 2% of the mortgage advance which was paid directly to the bank's mortgage specialist of these 'regulated' financial institutions.

Canada's housing market in 2017 was a classic bubble, specifically focussed in the Toronto and Vancouver areas.

In addition to historically low interest rates, through mortgage default insurance provided by Canada Mortgage and Housing Corporation, where the government guarantees lenders will be made whole in the event of a borrower default, fiscal policy has also supported the housing bubble.

The top of the Canadian housing market was triggered by a combination of regulatory changes and interest rates increases that have caused a debt servicing squeeze and this has impacted house prices. As lenders begin to worry about repayment, borrowers face higher interest rates or less available credit. Spending in the economy slows and the bull market now begins to play in reverse.

Looking at average numbers of debt to income (or debt service costs to income) for the economy fails to capture if risk is concentrated in certain sectors and here is where Canada is especially vulnerable.

Canada's construction and real estate employment sector now makes up a greater portion of the economy than at any time in Canadian history, residential investment as % of GDP is within spitting distance of historic highs. These developments are a notable issue for 2 reasons.

First, for the construction sector to continue to grow in line with the economy, bigger projects will need to be built in the future. Consider a builder who constructs 200 homes one year will need to build 204 homes to grow 2%, roughly in line with the economy.

If fewer homes are in demand, meaning investors and end users don't need more homes, the workers and suppliers are quickly impacted.

In the United States, fewer homes have been built each year

since the financial crisis of any year prior to 2008. The only exception was 1983 a time when interest rates approached 25%.

As housing construction projects approach completion housing, including of course condos, supply is expected to increase significantly over the coming years. This will lead to additional selling especially as speculative investors find it much harder to get mortgages and can only do so at much higher interest rates.

Borrowers who extended themselves, often with the help of banks creating mortgage income documentation may find themselves unable to service the mortgages.

Then there is Simone and thousands like her in the GTA and GVA, which is why anyone who expects a soft landing in the Canadian housing is more likely to find a rainbow unicorn.

Chapter 4

Investment Basics

Before we get into different investments and opportunities to reducing your investment management fees and taxes, its important to consider why invest in the first place.

Perhaps some of the best reasons to invest are the prospect of not having to work your entire life (retirement), to achieve financial security, and achieve other long-term financial goals (children's education, travel, cottage, sabbatical etc.)

In order to achieve those goals, it is important to recognize that there are only two ways to make money: by working and/or by having your money and assets work for you. If you keep your money under your mattress instead of investing it, you will never have more money than what you save. By investing, there are two ways your money can work for you

- Your money earns money. Someone pays you to use your money for a period of time. You then get your money back plus "interest." Or, if you buy stock in a company that pays "dividends" to shareholders, the company pays you a portion of its earnings on a regular basis. Now your money is making an "income."

- You buy something with your money that could increase in value. You become an owner of something (real estate or securities) that you hope increases in value over time. When you need your money back, you sell the asset, hoping someone will pay you more for it. In this case, your money is making a "capital gain".

Compound interest is a key feature of investing. With compound interest, over time you earn money on the money you've saved and in addition, earn money on the income or capital gain that your money has already earn earned. Over time with the power of compounding, even a small amount of savings can add up to big money and help you achieve your financial goals.

All investments involve some degree of risk. If you intend to purchase stocks, bonds, or real estate, it's important that you understand before you invest that you could lose some or all of your money. That remains true even if you purchase the investments through a bank.

The reward for taking on risk is the potential for a greater investment returns. If you have a financial goal with a long-term horizon, you can make more money by carefully investing in a low-cost diversified portfolio than a guaranteed investment certificate (GIC) or savings account. On the other hand, investing in short term, low yielding, safe investments may be appropriate for short-term (less than 3-5 year) financial goals.

So, the first questions around your investments is always what is your goal (s)?

The second important question is who can you trust to help you achieve those goals? With your existing advisor, are the fees you are paying for your investments clearly disclosed and understood? Do you know how your investment advisor is compensated?

Suitability Vs. Fiduciary Standard?

It's hard for most Canadians to imagine debating the merits and faults of a financial system that would ensure client interests are put first. The fiduciary standard has already been adopted in the UK and Australia, and most Canadians already believe their financial 'advisor' is required to put client interests first. The truth is that most financial 'advisors' in Canada are not required to put client interests first. Review the Regulatory Capture section in Chapter 3 for more information.

A fiduciary standard requires investment advisors put their client's interests above their own. It consists of a duty of loyalty and care, and simply means that the advisor must act in the best interest of his client.

In Canada, a bank employee does not meet this standard since the advisor's primary duty is to his employer, not their clients. Do you really think that Canadian banks generate record profit each year by putting their client interest above their own?

In Canada, the majority of the investment industry is made up of commissioned salespeople who only have to fulfill a suitability obligation. The suitability standard advisor has to reasonably believe that any recommendations made are suitable for clients, in terms of the client's financial needs, objectives and circumstances.

Your financial advisor may claim that your investments are suitable, knowing full well that better investment alternatives exist. For example, banks will often suggest investing in a Canadian

Equity fund when an index fund or ETF can provide better returns with lower risk since they have much lower fees.

In the world of investments, there is a constant conflict with your interests and improving your investment firm's bottom line. Basically, it is hard to get conflict free advice when your financial advisor's compensation is directly tied to selling you more expensive products and services.

Chartered Financial Analysts (CFA) are bound by the CFA Code or Ethics and a fiduciary responsibility to clients. A CFA has both a legal and ethical responsibility to clients based on trust and should be considered a minimum qualifications for someone who is qualified to discuss your investments.

How do you know if your financial plan is on track?

If you have questions about your current investments, we are happy to provide an independent assessment of your investments. An independent assessment either bring our clients peace of mind or identifies issues that will significantly affect their ability to achieve their goals.

We regularly encounter three major areas where investment plans go off track.

Fees – The fees you pay are one of the primary determinants of your investment returns. Fees have the impact of reducing the value of your investments and many clients underestimate the impact that these fees have over time. Investment returns can be variable, but fees will be charged regardless. But just as in buying cars, home appliances, or a mortgage, costs should play a role in your purchasing decision.

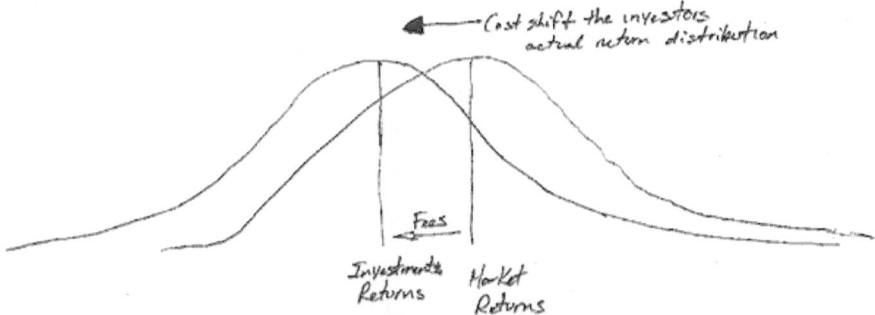

Cost shift the investors actual return distribution

Fees

Investment Returns *Market Returns*

Impact of Fees on Performance

Asset Allocation – Asset Allocation is an investment strategy that aims to balance risk and reward by apportioning a portfolio's assets according to an individual's goals, risk tolerance and investment horizon. Asset allocation is one of the most important decisions that investors make.

Investment Performance – Investment returns are variable over time but it is important to understand how your investments have performed relative to similar investments over time. Having an appropriate benchmark and comparing your investment results to this benchmark allows investors to gauge the relative performance of their investment portfolio.

A benchmark is a standard against which the performance of a security, mutual fund or investment manager can be measured. Generally, broad market and market-segment stock and bond indexes are used for this purpose. For example, a US equity manager or a US index fund would be compared to Standard & Poor's 500 Index.

Asset Allocation Basics

Asset allocation is an investment strategy that attempts to balance risk versus reward by adjusting the percentage of each asset in an investment portfolio according to the investor's risk tolerance, goals and investment time frame.

Financial experts generally agree that asset allocation is an important factor in determining returns for an investment portfolio. Asset allocation is based on the principle of diversification, that different assets perform differently in different market and economic conditions. Different asset classes offer returns that are not perfectly correlated. For example when stocks go up, bonds may go down and vice versa.

- Stocks: Stocks represent an ownership stake in an underlying business, and offer the highest return but also have historically had the highest volatility. There are many different kinds of stocks including dividend stock, growth stocks, domestic stocks, foreign stocks, emerging market stock and each offers different characteristics. In addition there are different market sectors including utilities, telecommunications, materials, information technology, industrials, health care, financials, energy, consumer staples and consumer sectors. Each type of stock and each market sector offers investors opportunities to diversify their portfolio.
- Bonds: When companies, governments or other large organization borrow money they often do so by selling bonds to investors. There are different types of bonds including government bonds, investment-grade or junk bonds; short-term, intermediate, long-term; domestic, foreign, and emerging markets bonds. Typically bonds offer lower returns than stocks and less volatility.
- Cash and cash equivalents (e.g., deposit account, money market fund).

Allocation among these three asset classes provides a starting point. In addition, investors can also have exposure to other asset classes. For example, many investors have allocations to real estate either through home ownership, rental properties, or REIT's (Real Estate Investment Trusts).

How to Invest

The most important rule of investing that I've learned in 20 years of personal and professional experience advising institutional and retail investors, an Honors degree in Economics from Queens University and Chartered Financial Analyst Designation is that if an investment is complicated or expensive, it should be avoided.

Passive management (also called indexing) is a portfolio management strategy based on purchasing exactly the same stocks and bonds, in the same proportions, as an index. Indexing doesn't entail any forecasting, so any use of market timing or stock picking would not qualify as passive management. An index strategy is implemented by simply purchasing securities in the same proportions as the market index.

By tracking an index, the idea is to minimize investment fees with an investment portfolio that provides diversification, low turnover, lowers taxes, and lower management fees. In the long term, the investor will have performance equal to the market average and investors benefit more from reducing investment costs than from trying to beat the averages.

Very few active investment managers outperform passively managed portfolios over long periods of time, especially after fees and taxes.

As passive management, index funds, and ETF's grow in

popularity the distinction between active and passive management is become much less clear. These specialized funds and closet active manager's offer specialized products sold as "ETFs" to capitalize on popularity of these investment vehicles and many charge higher management fees.

But what about Mutual Funds – isn't it the same?

A mutual fund is an investment vehicle that is made up of a pool of funds collected from many investors for the purpose of investing in securities such as stocks, bonds, money market instruments and similar assets. Mutual funds are operated by money managers, who invest the fund's capital and attempt to produce capital gains and income for the fund's investors. A mutual fund's portfolio is structured and maintained to match the investment objectives stated in its prospectus.

One of the main advantages of mutual funds is that they give small investors access to professionally managed, diversified portfolios of equities, bonds and other securities, which would be quite difficult to create with a small amount of capital.

Fees Matter

Minimizing cost is a critical part of every investor's toolkit. This is because in investing, there is no reason to assume that you get more if you pay more. Instead, every dollar paid for management fees, sales charges, and trading commissions is simply a dollar less earning potential return (and less money for your retirement or other financial goals). The more fees paid for someone to manage your funds, the smaller the amount left for you.

In a good markets investors have a tendency to ignore fees and in challenging markets they are scrutinized, but in the end no matter what type of market we are in fees do matter. The fees paid on the mutual funds directly impact how much the portfolio is worth at the end of the day.

The following chart, from the Ontario Securities Commission, shows the impact of fees on long term investment performance.

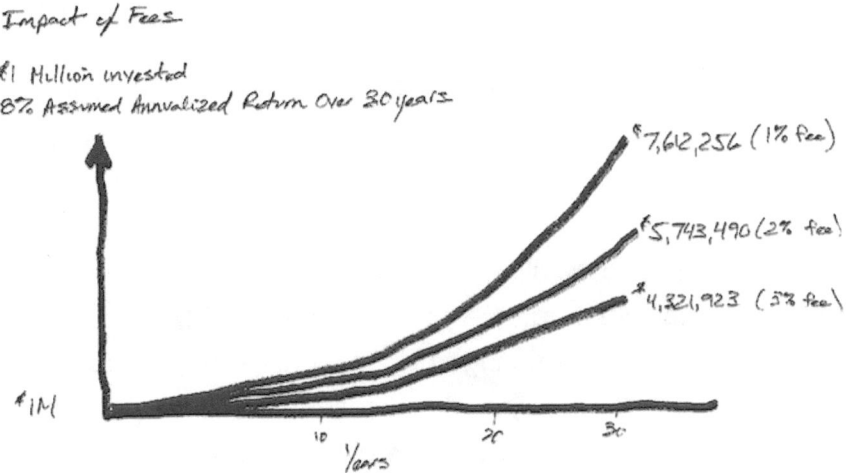

Impact of Fees Growth

Fees reduce the return you receive on your investments in mutual funds. The impact of recurring fees can be astounding and small differences in fees can translate into large differences over time, again due to the power of compounding. In Canada, you can find information about fees in a mutual fund's Fund Facts. Mutual fund companies are required to deliver a Fund Facts document within 2 days of buying a mutual fund. Fund fact documents can also be found online.

Since Canada has the highest mutual fund fees in the world, it is important to be aware of these fees:

The fund's management fee and operating expenses make up a fund's management expense ratio or MER. These are paid by you, through the fund, and expressed as an annual percentage of the total value of the fund. MERs can range from less than 1% to more than 3% these expenses will reduce the fund's returns each year by that percentage amount.

The management fee paid to the fund management company is to pay for overseeing the fund, hiring a portfolio manager to make the investment decisions, hiring other companies to assist in the administration of the fund, and trailing commission to your financial advisors firm's. Trailing commissions have been banned and are now illegal in much of the world, but not Canada. Operating expenses include bookkeeping and administrative fees, marketing costs, filings with the provincial securities commissions, legal fees, audit fees, custodian fees, GST/HST.

In addition to the management expense ratio, the fund will pay trading costs to buy and sell securities. Trading costs are expressed as an annual percentage of the total value of the fund known as the trading expense ratio.

Together the management expense ratio and trading expense ratio are the funds expenses, usually expressed as an annual percentage. To calculate the amount you are actually paying to invest in a mutual fund, simply multiply the amount you have invested by the fund expenses. For example a mutual fund investor with $300,000 invested at an average fund expense ratio of 2.75% will pay $8,250 each year in fund expenses. (The investors return will be $8,250 lower than the investments themselves returned)

Sales Charges – "Load of what?"

With mutual funds, you may also pay a sales charge when you buy or sell units or shares of a fund. Funds may be offered with a front-end load, back-end load, low load or no load. Loads in this case do not refer to cargo but are additional fees that you pay as an investor.

Mutual funds also charge clients additional administrative fees including switching fees, short-term trading fees, redemption fees, account fees, registered plan fees, and minimum account balance fees.

In Summary

Fees are something that each investor can control and each year these can reduce your return, and over time these recurring mutual fund fees can easily reduce your retirement portfolio by 30-50%. Having an easy to understand and transparent fee structure allows investors to understand what is being charged.

For this reason, I always recommend that clients invest in Index Funds. Over time, investors will be well served with a diversified portfolio with much lower cost than with traditional mutual funds in addition to tax efficiency through passive investments. In addition, a fee for advice service model allows fees to be tax deductible when paid separately from the fee charged by a fund. It also aligns your interests as a client, with those of your advisor.

Chapter 5

Investing

There are a couple developments over recent decades that have changed the investment landscape in Canada and globally. Many Canadian are applying financial advice that may have worked in the 80' and 90's to current financial planning and wondering why the results are disappointing.

I am assuming that you aren't using a cellphone or car from the 80's or 90's as technology has changed for the better. The investing landscape has also changed. Gone are many of the defined benefit pension plan and gone are the days where traditional investing options like mutual funds are enough to fund a retirement. In addition, expected returns from various financial markets have changed greatly in the last 30-40 years.

Bonds

There was a time that bonds provided investors an effective way to reduce market risk, generate income, and diversify an investment portfolio. Today, bonds are no longer a viable vehicle for growth or even a safety mechanism to protect against inflation. There are risks involved in purchasing even the safest government bonds including interest rates, inflation, and taxes.

First, when interest rates go up, the price of bonds falls.

A 5-year government of Canada bond yield is about 1.80% and inflation has averaged 2% in Canada since the Bank of Canada adopted a 1-3% inflation target in 1991. Bond 'investors' are almost guaranteed that purchasing power will fall by owning bonds as there are many good reasons to continue to expect inflation will continue to average 2% in Canada going forward.

As for taxes, outside of registered plans bond interest is taxed as regular income, unfavorably compared to capital gains or dividends.

Many factors have combined to lead to unprecedented demand for bonds in recent years. To maintain record low interest rates the US Federal Reserve, European Central Bank and Bank of Japan have been buying government bonds in order to increase demand and decrease interest rates.

Other central banks purchase bonds to diversify their central bank reserves and to keep their exchange rates competitive. These developments are both an unprecedented and likely unsustainable demand for bonds.

Finally, there has been tremendous demographic driven demand for bonds from income-oriented investors, as the population in developed markets continues to age and seek 'safe' sources of retirement income.

It shouldn't surprise anyone that buying bonds is effectively tying an anchor to the returns you can expect from your investment portfolio with current yields. Since many Canadians access financial markets through the highest cost mutual funds in the world, where fees often exceed 2%, your mutual funds company and mutual fund sales person are the only ones who have any realistic chance of profiting from your bond investments.

Why would your investment advisor suggest paying 2% fee to buy an investment that will generate an expected return of 1.80% before fees? Because, your advisor isn't paid on cash you have or if you leave your money in a safety deposit box or under your mattress.

Opportunity

Thankfully change also creates opportunity and what low bond yields have created are inexpensive ways for Canadians to borrow money. From my perspective as mortgage broker, investment advisor, and tax planner is that the re-advanceable mortgages available to Canadian homeowners today are the most powerful new financial instruments available to the average Canadian since RRSP's were introduced.

The first step is to take advantage of a re-advanceable mortgage, and the second step is to invest the funds in a safe, tax efficient, diversified portfolio. Together these steps enable today's investors to build wealth in a way that impossible for previous generations, but it does require some financial knowledge.

The bonus is the tax deductibility of interest, which dramatically minimizes the risk of borrowing to invest.

Now I realize that many people reading this book are focussed on paying down their mortgage, and becoming debt free, and then starting to save for retirement. Many people believe that borrowing to invest is risky. For most it is far riskier to not borrow to invest.

I have included 3 examples in a later chapter of clients accessing home equity to catch up on unused RRSP contributions, to invest in unregistered income producing investments, and to use an interest deduction to offset RRSP withdrawals to show how you can take advantage of this opportunity. But before we get to those strategies are two concepts that are crucial to understanding why this works.

Risk

Higher interest Rates

One risk of a borrowing to invest strategy would be that interest rates could shoot higher. The reality is that in Canada's governments and consumers are addicted to debt. Higher interest rates hurt consumers and government and for that reason we are unlikely to see significantly higher interest rates. As someone who spend 15 year advising the largest corporation, investment managers, and pension funds manage interest rate risk, I believe it is more likely that we see quantitative easing in Canada before we see an overnight rate of 5%.

Every month I see another report showing consumer debt (including mortgages) has never been higher in Canada, Ontario has the largest amount of debt of any non-sovereign borrower in the world, and despite strong and stable Canadian economy the federal government continues to run a significant deficit and record debt levels.

Today we are starting to see the housing market turn over in major centers after the Bank of Canada increased rates from 0.5% to 1.75% over that last 2 years, its hard to imagine what significantly higher interest rates would do the Canadian economy, which has become so dependent on construction and real estate related employment.

By borrowing to invest, you are hedged from higher interest

rates. Here's how – in Ontario once you earn over $95,000 annually your marginal tax rate is 43.41% and your marginal tax rate reaches 53.53% if your income exceeds $220,000.

Since money you've borrowed to invest is tax deductible, if you borrowed money at 4%, the tax deduction effectively means that investors in these tax brackets will be paying 2.2636% (4% * [1-0.4341]) or 1.8588% (4% * [1-0.4341]) after tax.

If interest rates increase to 5% everyone is paying 1% higher interest, except those that are borrowing to invest. After tax interest rates only increase by 0.5641% or 0.4747% for the investors described above.

In Canada we live in a society in which borrowing to buy a car is considered normal and borrowing to invest in wealth creating assets is considered risky. Some people might reasonably say that you might lose all your money if you borrow to invest, and that is certainly possible if you are thinking about investing in bitcoin or marijuana stocks.

A word on gold (or bitcoin)

The second major category of investments involves assets that will never produce anything, but that are purchased in the buyer's hope that someone else – who also knows that the assets will be forever unproductive – will pay more for them in the future. Tulips, of all things, briefly became a favorite of such buyers in the 17th century.

This type of investment requires an expanding pool of buyers, who, in turn, are enticed because they believe the buying pool will expand still further. Owners

*are not inspired by what the asset itself can produce –
it will remain lifeless forever – but rather by the belief
that others will desire it even more avidly in the future.*

*The major asset in this category is gold, currently a
huge favorite of investors who fear almost all other
assets, especially paper money (of whose value, as
noted, they are right to be fearful). Gold, however,
has two significant shortcomings, being neither of
much use nor procreative. True, gold has some indus-
trial and decorative utility, but the demand for these
purposes is both limited and incapable of soaking up
new production. Meanwhile, if you own one ounce
of gold for an eternity, you will still own one ounce
at its end.*

*What motivates most gold purchasers is their belief
that the ranks of the fearful will grow. During the past
decade that belief has proved correct. Beyond that,
the rising price has on its own generated additional
buying enthusiasm, attracting purchasers who see
the rise as validating an investment thesis.*

*As "bandwagon" investors join any party, they cre-
ate their own truth – for a while. Over the past 15
years, both Internet stocks and houses have demon-
strated the extraordinary excesses that can be created by combining an initially sensible thesis with
well-publicized rising prices. In these bubbles, an
army of originally skeptical investors succumbed to
the "proof" delivered by the market, and the pool of
buyers – for a time – expanded sufficiently to keep the*

bandwagon rolling. But bubbles blown large enough inevitably pop. And then the old proverb is confirmed once again: "What the wise man does in the beginning, the fool does in the end."

Today the world's gold stock is about 170,000 metric tons. If all of this gold were melded together, it would form a cube of about 68 feet per side. (Picture it fitting comfortably within a baseball infield.) At $1,750 per ounce – gold's price as I write this – its value would be $9.6 trillion. Call this cube pile A.

Let's now create a pile B costing an equal amount. For that, we could buy all U.S. cropland (400 million acres with output of about $200 billion annually), plus 16 Exxon Mobils (the world's most profitable company, one earning more than $40 billion annually). After these purchases, we would have about $1 trillion left over for walking-around money (no sense feeling strapped after this buying binge). Can you imagine an investor with $9.6 trillion selecting pile A over pile B?

Beyond the staggering valuation given the existing stock of gold, current prices make today's annual production of gold command about $160 billion. Buyers – whether jewelry and industrial users, frightened individuals, or speculators – must continually absorb this additional supply to merely maintain an equilibrium at present prices.

A century from now the 400 million acres of farm-land will have produced staggering amounts of corn, wheat, cotton, and other crops – and will continue to produce that valuable bounty, whatever the currency may be. Exxon Mobil will probably have delivered trillions of dollars in dividends to its owners and will also hold assets worth many more trillions (and, remember, you get 16 Exxons). The 170,000 tons of gold will be unchanged in size and still incapable of producing anything. You can fondle the cube, but it will not respond.

Admittedly, when people a century from now are fearful, it's likely many will still rush to gold. I'm confident, however, that the $9.6 trillion current valuation of pile A will compound over the century at a rate far inferior to that achieved by pile B.

Berkshire Hathaway, 2011 Annual Report

Global Equities

"Our favorite holding period is forever" – Warren Buffett

The reality is that a low cost, tax efficient, diversified portfolio will almost never lose money given a long enough time window. From year to year the S&P 500 (US stock market) goes up 73% of the time.

The worst one-year rolling time frame delivered a return of -43%. This occurred over the twelve months ending in February

2009. The best one-year index return delivered a 61% return, which occurred over the twelve months ending in June 1983.

If you were a long-term investor, the worst twenty years delivered a return of 6.4% a year. This occurred over the twenty years ending in May 1979. The best twenty years delivered an average return of 18% a year, which occurred over the twenty years ending in March 2000.

Over the long run as the economy grows, and earnings of companies grow, equity market returns become much less volatile.

Investors need to think about risk more broadly and include the concept of not meeting investment objectives and or losing purchasing power.

Opportunity Cost

Opportunity cost refers to the loss of potential gain from other alternatives when one alternative is chosen. Have you ever thought about how your life could have turned out with a different partner? That's opportunity cost.

With investing the choice is between investing and not investing. In this example your choice is clear, you could potentially borrow money from your home equity to invest or not.

By accessing your home equity and investing you get your money working in the market sooner, which is especially important for those that did not start investing early. Time value of money means that money available today is always worth more than the same amount of money in the future due to the power of compound interest.

Let's follow our example where someone decides to borrow to invest, by access $100,000 of dormant equity in their home, and the after-tax cost of borrowing is 2% due to the tax deductibility of interest.

If the $100,000 investment returns 6% annually, after 10 years the investment would be worth $179,084.77, after 20 years would be worth $320,713.54, after 30 years would be worth $574,349.12, and after 40 years would be worth $1,028,571.18.

If the $100,000 investment returns 8% annually, after 10 years the investment would be worth $215,892.25, after 20 years would be worth $466,095.71, after 30 years would be worth $1,006,265.69, and after 40 years would be worth $2,172,452.15.

Or the investor could not borrow to invest.

How much dormant equity do you have in your house?

Case Study – Tax Deductible Mortgage

Canada Revenue Agency allows you to deduct the interest portion of money borrowed to invest in unregistered investments, a business, or investment properties. If you have any of these investments, or plan on making any of these types of investments, it is possible to create audit trail for CRA compliance so that you can write off a portion (or all) of your mortgage interest.

It is important to understand that CRA's criteria is that purpose of the loan is to invest in income producing investments and this is quite easy to show if the investment is purchased directly from the proceeds of a loan. Even if that loan is secured by your primary residence.

I will leave it to your accountant to help if you are a business owner and focus on real estate investments and investments in financial markets.

Revisiting the great work Ray Dalio on debt and credit, the question on whether credit and debt growth is good or bad depends on what the credit produces and how the debt is repaid. Generally, because credit creates both spending power and debt, whether more credit is good depends on whether the borrowed money is used productively enough to generate enough income to service the debt.

If someone suggestion was to borrow money at current mortgage rates and invest in lower returning investments, it would be immediately clear to everyone that is not a great investment strategy.

For example, if you a borrowing at a 2% after tax cost and investing in bonds yielding 1.80% would clearly be a mistake as the investment wouldn't generate enough income to service the debt. The same argument would apply to gold and cash.

Investment Properties

Looking at real estate, one peculiarity that I have repeatedly encountered in my mortgage business is that real estate investors will purchase a house in Toronto for $1,000,000 and rent it out for $3,000/month. Meanwhile in many other Canadian markets, it is often a house that costs $300,000 that can be rented for $3,000/month.

I understand the benefits of tenants paying down a mortgage, and long-term appreciation that investors have come to expect by investing in Canadian real estate. However, these assumptions no longer make sense when borrowed money to buy an investment property does not generate enough income to service the debt.

Here's why?

Let assume the $1,000,000 property generates $36,000 in annual rents.

To maximize the interest deductibility the real estate investor would borrow the down payment from existing home equity through a re-advanceable mortgage and the rental property will ultimately be financed with a mortgage on the rental property.

Every day, I see seasoned real estate investors miss the opportunity deduct interest for both the down payment and mortgage for an investment property, costing themselves thousands each year - but this is the cost of getting mortgage advice from a real estate agent of bank teller.

Real estate investors would be better off using any amount saved for a down payment on a rental property to pay down their existing mortgage, and then re-borrow the money from home equity, in order to have the down payment recognized as an investment loan by CRA.

Assuming the investor could finance the rental purchase at an after-tax interest cost of $20,000 (assuming 2% after tax cost of $1M borrowed), the real estate investor also needs to consider the additional expenses including annual property taxes, repairs, insurance, allowance for vacancy, and potentially utilities. Considering all the expenses, it's hard to imagine how the investor would generate enough income to service the debt.

At best, the investor would expect a return of 0-1%, plus potentially the appreciation of the property. In addition, there can be cash flow issues from unexpected repairs and most mortgages need to be paid down, often requiring the investor put more money to the investment each month.

There have been times where investing in rental properties can make a lot of sense, but this is not one of those times in the GTA or GVA. Buying a property on the expectation that you can sell it to someone at a higher price, when it isn't a profitable investment (meaning it doesn't generate enough income to service the debt) at current prices is a foolish investment strategy. Ask anyone who invested in Bitcoin.

Investing in Global Equities

Stocks represent an ownership stake in an underlying business and offer the highest expected returns. There are many different kinds of stocks including dividend stock, growth stocks, domestic stocks, foreign stocks, emerging market stock and each offers different characteristics. In addition, there are different market sectors including utilities, telecommunications, materials, information technology, industrials, health care, financials, energy, consumer staples and consumer sectors. Each type of stock and each market sector offers investors opportunities to diversify their portfolio.

The are many global index funds that can provide investors diversification across many global markets and industries. As an example, the MSCI World Index captures representation from 23 Developed Market countries and includes 85% of the available investments in those countries.

The index returned 9.67% annualized for the 10 years ending December 31, 2018, currently pays a dividend yield of 2.76% and trades at approximately 16 times the earnings of the companies represented by the index.

The top 10 constituents of the index are companies that you've likely had of including Apple, Microsoft, Amazon, Johnson & Johnson, JPMorgan Chase, Alphabet (Google's parent company), Facebook, Exxon Mobile and Berkshire Hathaway.

When you invest in this index, you are buying shares in these businesses and the earnings they generate. At current prices, investor would be paying 16 times the earnings that the businesses generate. Initially this works out to an initial return of 6.25% (1/16th).

In addition, earnings of these businesses are almost certain to grow as these businesses reinvest the earnings that they do not pay out in dividends into the business.

If you want to take the view that the amount reinvested in the business has no value, global population growth an inflation virtually assures investors that revenues and earnings for these companies will grow in the future.

Borrowing at an after-tax cost of 2% to invest in assets earning 6.25% certainly seems more reasonable than investing in assets earning much lower returns (including bonds and Canadian real estate).

In addition, there are further advantages to using this strategy including the tax efficiency of the investments, the diversification benefits, and that these investments can be accessed at a very low cost (No real estate commission or land transfer tax).

Following our example where someone decides to borrow to invest, by access $100,000 of dormant equity in their home, and the after-tax cost of borrowing is 2% due to the tax deductibility of interest.

If the $100,000 investment returns 6% annually, after 10 years the investment would be worth $179,084.77, after 20 years would be worth $320,713.54, after 30 years would be worth $574,349.12, and after 40 years would be worth $1,028,571.18.

If the $100,000 investment returns 8% annually, after 10 years the investment would be worth $215,892.25, after 20 years would be worth $466,095.71, after 30 years would be worth $1,006,265.69, and after 40 years would be worth $2,172,452.15.

Again the lowest returns the S&P 500 generated over a 20 year period was 6.8%.

Of course, the investment loan would also grow to $121,899.44 after 10 years, $148,594.74 after 20 years, $181,136.16 over 30 years, and $220,803.97 after 40 years and would need to be repaid eventually.

Chapter 6

Retirement Tax Planning Guide 2019

"in this world nothing can be said to be certain, except **death and taxes**." —*Benjamin Franklin,*

In Canada, it is certainly possible to use planning to reduce your taxes significantly and this is a primary focus of my financial planning practice. By helping clients reduce their taxes and reduce the fees they pay for investments, I help clients have significantly more money in retirement.

As I updated my Retirement Tax Planning Guide to reflects 2019's retirement realities, it remains clear that change is a constant in retirement planning and for this reason it is especially important to work with a trusted advisor to review your investment goals and personal situation annually.

Canadians have many ways to pay for retirement – from private pensions, government pensions (Canada Pension Plan and Old Age Security), to RRSP/RRIF's and home equity. The intention of this guide is to provide options and identify opportunities so that you keep more of your retirement nest egg from the taxman.

In the three years, since I originally wrote the Retirement Tax

Planning Guide – Canada Pension Plan has been changed considerably to reflect the reality that fewer workers are covered by pension plans each year. Today's CPP is designed to replace 25 percent of your income and by 2065, with these changes, CPP is designed to replace 33.3% of your income, up to a limit. CPP contribution levels for employers and employees will increase from 2019 to 2023 to accommodate for the increased future benefits.

Canadians continue to be eligible for Old Age Security at age 65 – this age was set to increase to age 67.

Personal income tax rates have increased for those earning high incomes and personal income tax rates have decreased for medium and lower income earners, making tax planning more important.

I have organized the guide into a couple sections -

- Taxes and strategies to reduce your taxes in retirement
- Strategies to maximize your pension benefits
- Strategies to maximize the after tax value of your investments.

I am very confident that we can improve your investment results and reduce the taxes you pay in retirement

Please contact me with any questions or feedback.

Kevin Bell, CFA
kevin@kevinbell.ca
416-769-1440

Tax bracket top up

Einstein said that the hardest thing in the world to understand is income taxes.

Retirement tax planning often requires a shift in mindset

from tax planning for most working Canadian. For many working Canadians, RRSPs have created a mindset of deferring income for as long as possible. Approaching retirement, it is important to realize that deferring income will only continue to make sense if you are in a lower tax bracket in retirement.

The idea of tax bracket "top up" in retirement is to keep your retirement income taxed at the lowest rates ***throughout your entire retirement***. Ultimately this is a budgeting decision with an idea of your available retirement resources, how much income you need to support your lifestyle, and determining how to keep your taxable income below the next income tax threshold each year in order to reduce your average tax rate over your entire retirement.

Below are the combined Federal & Ontario personal marginal tax rates for 2018

- 20.05% **on the first** $43,906 of taxable income
- 24.15% over $43,906 up to $47,630
- 29.65% over $47,630 up to $77,313
- 31.48% over $77,313 up to $87,813 (+ 15% for OAS claw back = 46.48%)
- 33.89% over $87,813 up to $91,101 (+ 15% for OAS claw back = 48.89%)
- 37.91% over $91,101 up to $95,259 (+ 15% for OAS claw back = 52.91%)
- 43.41% over $95,259 up to $147,667 (up to $121,314 add 15% for OAS claw back = 58.41%)
- 46.41% over $147,667 up to $150,000
- 47.97% over $150,000 up to $200,000
- 51.97% over $200,000 up to $220,000
- 53.53% over $220,000

Old Age Security is subject to a claw back provision which limits the amount received for higher income earners. For every dollar over the threshold ($74,788 in 2018), $0.15 is clawed back. Once your income exceeds $121,314, 100% of your OAS pension will be clawed back. The claw back must be included in determining the tax rates you expect to pay in retirement. Turns out even if you call something a claw back, it is still a tax.

Incredibly, the highest effective marginal personal tax rates in Ontario are seniors receiving Old Age Security, with incomes between $95,259 and $121,314 at 58.41% (and that doesn't include property tax, sales tax, gas tax, etc., but don't get me started)

Government Pensions

Canada Pension Plan

In 2018, maximum monthly Canada Pension Plan (CPP) payments were $1,134.17 for someone electing to begin receiving CPP at 65. This will be increased by about 2% (about $20/month) beginning January 2019

With CPP, Canadians can elect to begin receiving payments at age 60 or defer their pension as late as age 70. The early and late withdrawal rules work like this:

- If you take CPP *before age 65*, you take a *7.2%* penalty per year on your CPP payments. The reduction to your monthly CPP payments is *36%* if you elect to start payments at age 60. The maximum monthly pension is $725.87 starting at age 60. Age 60 is the earliest point at which you are eligible to start taking CPP.
- If you take CPP *after age 65*, you receive an addition *8.4%* increase per year on your CPP payments. The increase to

your monthly CPP payments is *42%* if you elect to start payments at age 70. The maximum monthly pension is $1,610.52 starting at age 70. Age 70 is the latest point at which you can start taking CPP.

When should I apply for my Canada Pension Plan benefits?

Will you live long enough to capitalize on the larger payments, if you wait to start taking CPP later? Are you going to receive more **after tax** CPP income by waiting?

The answer depends on three assumptions - how long you will live, the rate of return you expect to earn on your money, and your retirement tax rates.

Currently, according to Statistics Canada, a man at age 60 can expect to live another 23 years (age 83), and a woman about 26 (age 86). These are only "averages" and you should base your decision on the specifics of your own personal health situation. If you are a smoker, or in poor health, these average scenarios may not be applicable, likewise if longevity runs in your family and you are in perfect health the averages might not be appropriate.

Using the "averages", we can show that an average woman maximizes her total CPP payout by waiting until age 70 receiving *$290,304* payments from age 70 to age 86, instead of $268,380 starting at age 65, and $212,659.20 starting at age 60. A man maximizes his total CPP payout also by waiting until age 70 receiving in *$235,872* of payments from age 70 to age 83, instead of $230,040 starting at age 65, and $188,122 starting at age 60.

Since CPP payments are adjusted every January to reflect changes in the cost of living we are assuming real (inflation adjusted) CPP_payments, not nominal payments. The underlying assumption is that investments that you draw on from age 60 to 70 instead of CPP, would grow by the rate of inflation. If your investments grow faster than inflation (after tax) there may be another reason to take CPP early. Conversely, if your other investment sources are likely to grow less than inflation, after taxes, taking CPP early might make sense.

Finally, taxation also plays an important role in your decision on when to take CPP. Canada Pension Plan income is fully taxable and needs to be included in a plan to maximize **after tax** income throughout retirement. With our calculations above, we are assuming that retirees are facing the same marginal tax rates on CPP income throughout retirement and this is not always the case.

Old Age Security

A report from the federal Task Force on Financial Literacy said that roughly 160,000 eligible seniors do not receive Old Age Security (OAS) benefits. This represents almost $1-billion in benefits that are unclaimed annually. Canadians need to apply for Old Age Security benefits, and apparently many do not.

Canadians can defer OAS pension for a maximum of 60 months past age 65, in exchange for a higher monthly Old Age Security pension. For every month you delay receipt of your OAS pension, your payment will be increased by 0.6%, from $586.66/month at age 65 to a maximum at age 70 of $797.86/month (36% higher). There is no option to take OAS earlier than age 65.

When should I apply for my Old Age Security (OAS) benefits at age 65 or 70?

Looking at the math, the total lifetime Old Age Security pension received is greater just before the pensioner reaches the age of 84 if you defer the pension from age 65 to age 70. According to statistics Canada, a man at age 65 can expect to live another 19 years (age 84), and a woman about 22 (age 87). These breakeven ages are much later than the deferral breakeven for Canada Pension Plan.

With significantly higher breakeven ages for OAS than CPP, is there any value in deferring Old Age Security?

There are still a few reasons that someone may want to defer their OAS pension and the deferral decision depends on the same three assumptions about a retiree's personal circumstances as CPP - how long you expect to live, the rate of return you expect to earn on your money, and your retirement tax rates.

You should base your decision on the specifics of your own personal health situation. If you are in great shape and have longevity in your family, these average life expectancy scenarios may not be applicable. In these cases, it can make sense to defer your OAS.

The decision is also impacted by the amount you could earn on your money. If you expect to generate a higher return than inflation, it may make additional economic sense to take OAS at 65 to increase the value of other investments

For most retiree, the decision has to do with income taxes. If you are still working at or after age 65, your OAS pension may be taxed at a higher rate than after you stop working. Tax planning in retirement should be used to reduce the overall rate of taxes over your entire retirement, which is different than the decision to defer taxes in your working years. Deferring taxes in retirement doesn't make sense if you will be paying a higher tax rate on deferred income, which is especially important with Old Age Security.

Old Age Security is subject to a claw back provision which limits the benefit received for higher income earners. For every dollar over the threshold ($74,788 in 2018), $0.15 is clawed back. Once your income exceeds $121,314, 100% of your OAS pension will be clawed back. The 15% income claw back must be included in determining the tax rates you expect to pay in retirement.

Dividend Gross Up (and Eliminating Old Age Security Claw Back)

The Old Age Security claw back is a big issue because it is effectively an additional 15% income tax on top of the current marginal tax rates. According to Human Resource Development Canada, only about five percent of seniors receive reduced OAS pensions, and only two percent lose the entire amount.

In terms of planning, if you are one of these people who face losing some of the OAS due to claw back because your income over the age of 65 will be higher than $74,788, then you can consider some simple strategies to help you minimize the claw back.

1. **Spend RRSPs before you turn 65.** One of the benefits of <u>investing in RRSPs</u> is that it is a tax deferral. And while tax deferral is great, it is only good when you are paying the same or less tax in retirement. If you under 65 and in a lower tax bracket than you will be in retirement, it makes sense to withdraw from your RRSP.

2. **Income splitting in retirement.** With pension splitting, spouses can give up to 50% of their pension income to their spouse for tax splitting purposes. This is a very effective way to reduce income if you are close to the OAS claw back threshold. For retirees with no pension income, <u>RRIF</u> and annuity income qualify for pension splitting after the age of 65. In addition, you can use your spouse's age to calculate the minimum amount that you must withdrawal from a RRIF. Splitting or sharing Canada Pension Plan (CPP) is another <u>income splitting strategy</u> that can help minimize or avoid OAS claw back.

3. **Tax efficient income on non-RRSP investments.** When it comes to investment income from non-registered investments, different types of income are taxed differently. It may be more effective to seek capital gains (and realize gains strategically) as opposed to dividend and interest income.

4. **Dividend income.** The problem with dividend income is the process to getting a tax break includes a dividend gross up before the application of the dividend tax credit. As a result, dividend income can actually get you closer to the OAS claw back threshold because the "grossed up" income is used. If you income is close to the OAS threshold, be especially careful about selecting investments that produce dividend income.

5. **Use Tax Free Savings Accounts (TFSA)** – <u>Tax free savings accounts</u> are favourable compared to non-registered investments simply because the investment income is non-taxable inside the TFSA. Maximizing the TFSA is a great strategy to reduce OAS claw back especially if the

investment income (dividends and interest) would put you over the OAS threshold.

6. **B**orrowing **to invest** can help reduce OAS claw back if the interest on the loan is tax deductible. This interest deductibility reduces your net income dollar-for-dollar, and at the end of the loan, you pay the principal on the loan and keep the after-tax investment income.

7. **Watch for capital dispositions after the age of 65.** Retirees with rental properties, cottages, or significant unrealized capital gains from investments may be better off triggering those gains before the age of 65 or strategically after beginning to receive OAS to avoid losing OAS benefits from claw back. One of the great advantage of having a portfolio that is focussed on capital gains is that the individual has a great deal of control over when these gains are realized (ideally never), compared to dividends and interest income.

Maximizing your Pension Income Tax Credit

Major trends are continuing to reshape Canadians pensions. The biggest issue is that employers are increasingly sharing or off-loading pension risk to employees (either through moving from defined benefits pensions to defined contribution pension or by eliminating pensions entirely). The result is that Canadians need to be increasingly aware of the opportunities available to ensure a comfortable retirement. It is not always what you earn that counts, it's often what you get to keep.

The Pension Income Tax credit is available to you if you are 55 years of age or older. Basically, it enables you to deduct, from taxes payable, a tax credit equal to the lesser of your pension income or $2,000.00.

Eligible pension income depends on your age. If you are between 55 and 65 pension income includes income from a superannuation or pension fund and annuity income arising from the death of your spouse under a RRSP, RRIF, DPSP. If you are 65 or older in the year, pension income is defined more broadly and includes income from a Registered Retirement Income Fund (RRIF), interest from a prescribed non-registered annuity, income from foreign pensions, and interest from a non-registered GIC offered by a life insurance company.

Investment income from market-based investments, interest income from GICs with banks, trust companies and credit unions, Old Age Security, Canada Pension Plan, lump sum death benefits, lump sum withdrawals from RRSPs, and retiring allowances are **not eligible pension** income.

If you are not part of a superannuation or pension plan, you are still able to create qualified pension income to save taxes. This can be accomplished by

1. **Transfer RRSP to a RRIF.** At age 65 transfer $12,000 to a RRIF and take $2000 out per year from age 65 to 71(inclusive). This essentially allows you to get $2000 out of your RRSP tax-free for 6 years. Whether you need the income or not, it is an opportunity you do not want to miss.

2. **Transfer Locked-in Retirement Account (LIRA) assets to a Life Income Fund (LIF) and then annuitize.** In most cases, you can transfer your LIRA to a LIF or LRIF once you reach the age of 55. To make the most of this strategy, you must transfer the LIRA to the LIF and then to an annuity in order for the income to be reported as eligible

pension income. If you purchase the annuity directly from the LIRA, the annuity is considered a RRSP annuity, which only qualifies for the pension income credit after age 65.

3. **Buy a GIC from a life insurance company.** If you do not have any qualifying pension income, are age 65 or over, and do not want to draw down your registered assets at this time, there is a relatively easy way to make a GIC qualify for the Pension Income Tax Credit. Simply purchase a GIC through a life insurance company because it is considered eligible pension income.

4. **Transfer of Unused Credit to a Spouse.** Unused pension income credit is transferable to a spouse or common-law partner. The ability to transfer this credit should be explored in circumstances where one spouse is earning pension income in excess of $2,000, and the other spouse is not otherwise fully utilizing his or her pension income credit.

If you are over the age of 65, take a look at line 314 in your tax return to see if you are taking advantage of the Pension Income Tax Credit. If not, consider one of these tax savings strategies.

Saving Tax on your Registered Retirement Income Fund (RRIF)

You can convert your RRSP holdings to a RRIF at any time. However, an RRSP must be converted to a RRIF, annuity, or paid out in a lump sum by the end of the calendar year that you turn age 71. If you convert your RRSP to a RRIF, payments are not required to begin until the calendar year following the year that the RRIF account was opened (the year you turn age 72).

A RRIF provides a high level of control over the investments in your retirement plan, the continued advantage of tax-free growth of assets within the plan, as well as maximum flexibility in establishing an income stream.

The federal government sets the minimum amount you must take out of your RRIF every year. It's based on a percentage of the value of your RRIF. Here's how it works:

- The minimum amount increases as you get older. For example, at 71 minimum withdrawal rate is 5.28%, increasing to 5.98% at age 76, 7.08% at age 81, 8.99% at age 86, and reaching a 20% withdrawal minimum at age 95.
- There is no maximum withdrawal limit, but all withdrawals are fully taxable income.
- You can choose to make regular monthly, quarterly, semi-annual or annual withdrawals.

If your spouse is younger than you, you can use your spouses age to calculate your minimum withdrawal amount. This is a good strategy if you have other sources of funds and want to leave your money in your RRIF to defer taxes for as long as possible. You must tell your financial institution that you're doing so before you make your first RRIF withdrawal. And you can't change your mind later, but you can set up multiple RRIF's for multiple purposes.

Since RRSP's & RRIF's can make up a significant portion of a retirement income plan it is important to understand that the goal of tax planning is to reduce taxes over your entire retirement, which is different than the primary goal of deferring taxes using an RRSP's during ones working years. Deferring taxes is generally a good idea, but not when you are deferring taxes to pay taxes at higher tax rate in the future.

Any remaining funds in your RRIF become taxable income on the date of your death. By having your estate realizing the remaining value of your RRSP or RRIF as income in a single year can result in significant taxes (think 50%). If you have a spouse, the funds in your RRIF can be transferred to an RRSP or RRIF of your spouse. There are some other cases such as with disabled and dependent children or grandchildren, where RRIF's can also be rolled over tax free.

*Note a (Life Income Fund) LIF is to a (Locked in Retirement Account) LIRA what a RRIF is to an RRSP, with one difference – Life Income Fund (LIF) withdrawals are subject to a maximum amount to ensure that your retirement income does not run out too quickly.

Withdrawing money tax free from your RRSP

An "RRSP meltdown" can be a very important strategy for clients looking to reduce taxable income in retirement. Specifically, if RRIF minimums will cause income to be taxed at a higher rate in retirement (or lose OAS benefits) the strategy can be used to withdraw funds from an RRSP "tax free" ahead of retirement. I have included an example of how this strategy can work below but each "meltdown" requires time and a personalized plan.

Essentially, by borrowing to invest in favorably taxed unregistered assets you can use an interest deduction to reduce your taxable income and offset the deduction by withdrawing money from registered plans before retirement.

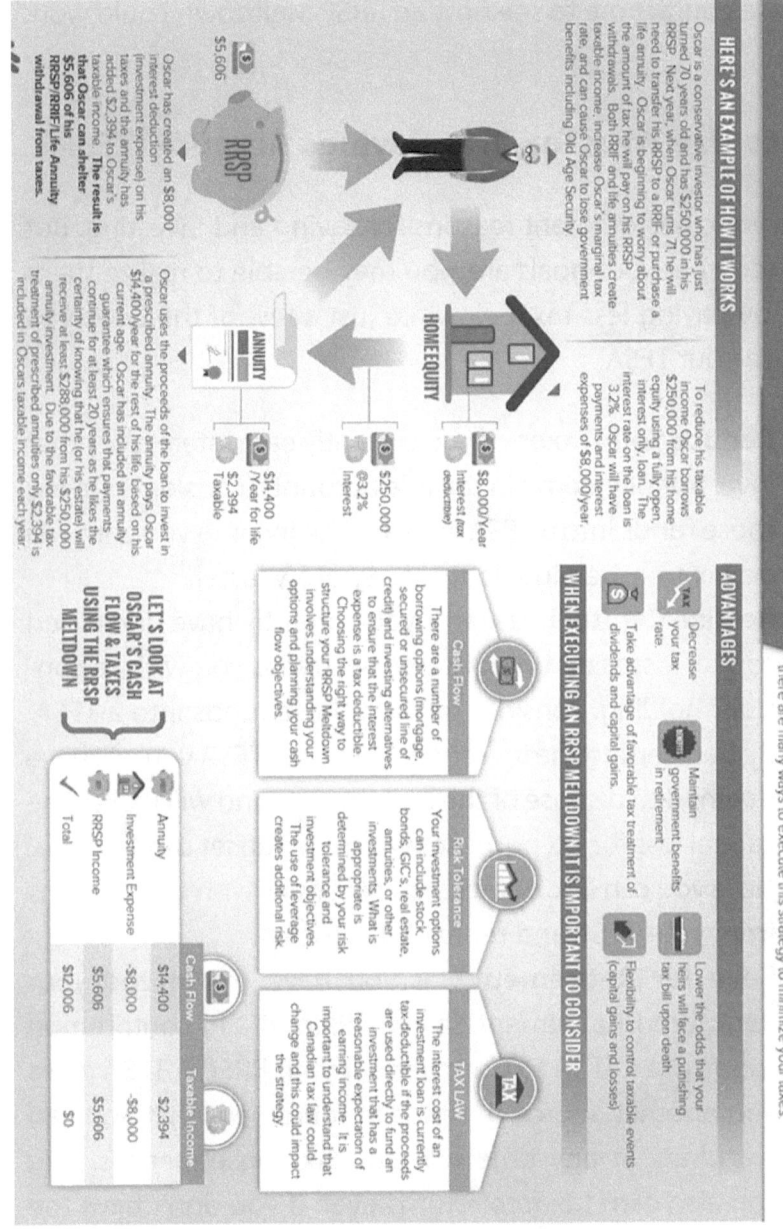

RRSP MELTDOWN

RRSP Meltdown is a strategy which can help Canadian's withdraw money from their RRSP without paying tax. By using the strategy, Canadians are offsetting the income of their RRSP/RRIF withdrawals with an interest expense deduction. Keep in mind that depending on your age and financial objectives, there are many ways to execute this strategy to minimize your taxes.

HERE'S AN EXAMPLE OF HOW IT WORKS

Oscar is a conservative investor who has just turned 70 years old and has $250,000 in his RRSP. Next year, when Oscar turns 71, he will need to transfer his RRSP to a RRIF or purchase a life annuity. Oscar is beginning to worry about the amount of tax he will pay on his RRSP withdrawals. Both RRIF and life annuities create taxable income, increase Oscar's marginal tax rate, and can cause Oscar to lose government benefits including Old Age Security.

To reduce his taxable income Oscar borrows $250,000 from his home equity using a fully open, interest only, loan. The interest rate on the loan is 3.2%. Oscar will have payments and interest expenses of $8,000/year.

$8,000/Year
Interest (tax deductible)

HOMEEQUITY

$250,000
@3.2%
Interest

$14,400
/Year for life
Taxable

$2,394
Taxable

ANNUITY

RRSP

$5,606

Oscar has created an $8,000 interest deduction (investment expense) on his taxes and the annuity has added $2,394 to Oscar's taxable income. **The result is that Oscar can shelter $5,606 of this RRSP/RRIF-Life Annuity withdrawal from taxes.**

Oscar uses the proceeds of the loan to invest in a prescribed annuity. The annuity pays Oscar $14,400/year for the rest of his life, based on his current age. Oscar has included an annuity guarantee which ensures that payments continue for at least 20 years as he likes the certainty of knowing that he (or his estate) will receive at least $288,000 from his $250,000 annuity investment. Due to the favorable tax treatment of prescribed annuities only $2,394 is included in Oscar's taxable income each year.

ADVANTAGES

Decrease your tax rate.

Maintain government benefits in retirement

Take advantage of favorable tax treatment of dividends and capital gains.

Lower the odds that your heirs will face a punishing tax bill upon death

Flexibility to control taxable events (capital gains and losses)

WHEN EXECUTING AN RRSP MELTDOWN IT IS IMPORTANT TO CONSIDER

Cash Flow
There are a number of borrowing options (mortgage, secured or unsecured line of credit) and investing alternatives to ensure that the interest expense is a tax deductible expense. Choosing the right way to structure your RRSP Meltdown involves understanding your options and planning your cash flow objectives.

Risk Tolerance
Your investment options can include stock, bonds, GICs, real estate, annuities, or other investments. What is appropriate is determined by your risk tolerance and investment objectives. The use of leverage creates additional risk.

TAX LAW
The interest cost of an investment loan is currently tax-deductible if the proceeds are used directly to fund an investment that has a reasonable expectation of earning income. It is important to understand that Canadian tax law could change and this could impact the strategy.

LET'S LOOK AT OSCAR'S CASH FLOW & TAXES USING THE RRSP MELTDOWN

	Cash Flow	Taxable Income
Annuity	$14,400	$2,394
Investment Expense	-$8,000	-$8,000
RRSP Income	$5,606	$5,606
Total	$12,006	$0

RRSP Meltdown

Please contact me to see how an RRSP Meltdown could work for you

Ways to Use Your Tax-Free Savings Account (TFSA)

Everyone has different reasons for saving and investing. But no matter what your goals are, you may be able to realize them sooner by paying less tax. Below are just a few of the ways you could use your TFSA.

- **Reduce Your Taxes** - If you currently earn interest or other investment income in taxable accounts, consider moving those funds into a TFSA instead. The income you earn will be tax-free, helping your money grow faster.
- **Realize Capital Losses** - If you currently have unrealized capital losses on unregistered securities you wish to consider holding, consider moving those funds into a TFSA. By transferring the investments to your TFSA you will have deemed to dispose of the investments and will realize the capital loss for tax purposes which can offset capital gains. Note you can also withdrawal securities with capital gains from your TFSA and repeat this process.
- **Save for Retirement** - If you have maximized your Registered Retirement Savings Plan (RRSP) contribution room, use a TFSA to complement your RRSP. A TFSA gives you another source of funds in retirement that you can withdraw at any time without tax consequences. You can also earn tax-free returns even if you don't have the earned income required to make an RRSP contribution. And you can contribute at any age once you become an adult.

- **Save During Retirement** - If you have a Registered Retirement Income Fund (RRIF), you are required to withdraw a minimum amount every year. If you don't need all of your RRIF withdrawal or pension income to cover your living expenses, you can contribute the excess to a TFSA where your funds can continue to enjoy tax-free compound growth.

- **Split Income with Your Spouse or Partner** - You can give funds to your spouse or common-law partner, who can then use them to contribute to his or her own TFSA. This can help to equalize your future incomes and has the potential to lower your family's overall tax bill. Returns earned inside the account are not attributed back to you so there is no tax consequence to either you or your spouse while the funds remain within the TFSA. Just note that the money in your spouse's TFSA belongs to your spouse.

- **Maintain Eligibility for Government Programs** - TFSA earnings and withdrawals are not included as income for tax purposes, so they don't affect your eligibility for income-tested government benefits and tax credits like Old Age Security (OAS) or the Goods and Services Tax (GST) credit.

Canada no longer has any form of estate or inheritance tax. Yet despite this, death can trigger a significant income tax bill that, if not properly planned for, can leave an unexpected liability when a loved one passes away. These issues can be dealt with more effectively through planning.

Here is what happens to your registered and non-registered assets when you die:

Registered Plans

For many Canadians, however, the largest tax liability their estate will face is the tax on the value of their RRSP or RRIF upon death. The tax rules require the fair market value of the RRSP or RRIF as of the date of death to be included <u>as income</u> on the deceased's terminal tax return, with tax payable at the deceased taxpayer's marginal tax rate for the year of death.

In Ontario, marginal tax rates jump from 20.05% on income less than $43,906 to 43.41% above $95,259 to 53.53% above $220,000.

This income inclusion can be deferred if the RRSP or RRIF is left to a surviving spouse or partner, in which case tax will be payable by the survivor at his or her marginal tax rate in the year in which funds are withdrawn from the RRSP or RRIF.

Non-Registered Assets

The general rule for non-registered assets is that a taxpayer is deemed to have disposed of all his or her property, such as stocks, bonds, mutual funds and real estate (including cottage) immediately before death at their fair market value (FMV).

When the FMV exceeds the property's adjusted cost base (ACB), the result is a capital gain, half of which is taxable to the deceased and must be reported in the deceased's final tax return, known as the "terminal return."

There is an exception for the capital gain arising on the deemed disposition upon death of your principal residence, which is generally tax exempt.

If you own qualified small business corporation (QSBC) shares, a qualified farm or fishing property upon death, you can claim on your terminal return any remaining lifetime capital gains exemption against any capital gains arising from the deemed disposition of that property.

Perhaps the best way to avoid or at least defer this deemed disposition upon death is to transfer the property to the deceased's spouse or partner, where applicable. When property is transferred in this way, the transfer can be done without triggering any immediate capital gains and the associated tax liability can be deferred until the death of the second spouse or partner (or until that spouse or partner sells the property, if earlier.)

Charitable Giving

Another opportunity to eliminate the tax arising from the deemed disposition at death is to consider leaving appreciated marketable securities to a registered charity through your will. The capital gains tax is completely eliminated when appreciated publicly listed shares, mutual funds or segregated funds are donated in-kind to charity.

In addition, a charitable donation receipt for the FMV of the shares donated upon death would be issued which could produce a tax savings on the terminal return (or in the prior year's return) of at least 40%, depending on his province of residence.

Life Insurance

Funding estate taxes through life insurance is the most efficient way and least costly way to preserve wealth from one generation to the next and avoid paying close to half of your retirement saving to the tax man when you die.

When you redirect a portion of your retirement savings to a tax exempt insurance policy, you can ensure that the pre-tax value of your retirement savings will go to the people and charities you care most.

About the Author

Kevin Bell has spent much of the last twenty years working on the trading floors of CIBC World Markets and Credit Suisse advising institutional investors, including Canada's largest companies, pension funds, and investment managers on how to manage financial risks. He operates The  Mortgage Group (www.kevinbell.ca) and helps clients secure the best mortgage possible while leveraging interest and tax savings. In addition, Kevin provides fee based investment advice through Portfolio Strategies Corporation. He graduated from Queens University with a degree in economics and earned his Chartered Financial Analyst designation in 2000.